CO-OPERATIVE CENTRALIZED PURCHASING

IN THE

CITY OF NEW YORK

RESULTS OF A YEAR'S PRACTICAL TEST OF CENTRAL PURCHASING IN THE MAYOR'S DEPARTMENTS

CONDUCTED BY THE
MAYOR'S CENTRAL PURCHASING COMMITTEE
1915

1837
ARTES
VERITAS
SCIENTIA
LIBRARY OF THE
UNIVERSITY OF MICHIGAN
TUEBOR
SI QUAERIS PENINSULAM AMOENAM
CIRCUMSPICE

CO-OPERATIVE CENTRALIZED PURCHASING

IN THE

CITY OF NEW YORK

RESULTS OF A YEAR'S PRACTICAL TEST OF CENTRAL PURCHASING IN THE MAYOR'S DEPARTMENTS

CONDUCTED BY THE
MAYOR'S CENTRAL PURCHASING COMMITTEE
1915

PRESS OF
CLARENCE S. NATHAN, INC.,
NEW YORK.

5639-15-1000 (N)

October 1, 1915.

HON. JOHN PURROY MITCHEL,
Mayor.

Sir:

In behalf of the Mayor's Central Purchasing Committee, I beg to submit herewith a record of the results of a year's practical test of co-operative centralized purchasing for the twenty-eight departments, boards and offices immediately under your control. This test has been made under the direction of the committee appointed by you in November, 1914, and is in active progress at the present time. Steps have already been taken to consolidate again the contract purchases of the mayor's departments during 1916.

Results obtained to date demonstrate that the present co-operative purchasing should be continued in some form. The suggestions offered in the accompanying report will, we are confident, be of service in developing a permanent central purchasing system for the city of New York.

I wish to emphasize particularly the effective work done by the secretary of the committee, Mr. Frederic R. Leach, who has been the immediate head of the central purchasing staff, and who has worked out the details of the constructive plan herewith presented. Mr. Leach succeeded in a remarkably short time, with no increased expenditure for services, in overcoming the many technical difficulties which stood in the way of the central co-operative purchasing undertaking.

In the conduct of this experiment your committee has received valuable and continuous assistance from the office of the commissioners of accounts, the finance department, the bureau of standards, the law department, the board of city record, the various commissioners and employees of the co-operating departments, the Bureau of Municipal Research, and a large number of manufacturers and dealers. The co-operation of the Bureau of Muncipal Research has been continuous and practical, and of marked value in the successful conduct of the experiment.

Respectfully Submitted,

HENRY BRUÈRE, Chairman,

CENTRAL PURCHASING COMMITTEE.

OFFICIALS, DEPARTMENTS AND AGENCIES PARTICIPATING IN THE TEST

HON. JOHN PURROY MITCHEL, Mayor

CO-OPERATING AGENCIES

Department of Finance
Office of the Commissioners of Accounts
Law Department
Bureau of Standards
Board of City Record
Bureau of Municipal Research

CENTRAL COMMITTEE

HENRY BRUÈRE, Chairman, Chamberlain
DAVID FERGUSON, Supervisor, Board of City Record
JAMES MCGINLEY, Chief of Staff, Commissioners of Accounts
GEORGE L. TIRRELL, Director, Bureau of Standards
FREDERIC R. LEACH, Secretary

ASSOCIATE COMMITTEE

(Composed of Purchasing Experts from the Co-operating Departments)

GEORGE A. WHITE,
ADOLPH H. WITSCHIEBEN,
Bellevue and Allied Hospitals

JAMES A. KINGSLEY,
FRANCIS W. PERRY,
Department of Bridges

F. F. C. RIPPON,
Department of Correction

HAROLD CLEMENS,
Department of Docks and Ferries

JOHN R. KEEFE,
Fire Department

HENRY A. SCHICKLING,
Department of Health

L. J. MCDERMOTT,
Police Department

JOHN MCCARTHY,
Department of Parks,
Manhattan and Richmond

ROBERT T. FLYNN,
Department of Parks,
Brooklyn

EUGENE C. BAGWELL,
Department of Parks, Bronx

IRWIN THOMAS,
Department of Parks, Queens

JAMES T. DEVLIN,
JOHN J. O'BRIEN,
Department of Street Cleaning

EDMOND BEARDSLEY,
FRANK H. WARDER,
Department of Water Supply,
Gas and Electricity

FREDERICK J. KENNEY HENRY F. SCHEITLIN
Department of Public Charities

PARTICIPATING DEPARTMENTS

Bellevue and Allied Hospitals
Department of Bridges
Department of Correction
Department of Docks and Ferries
Fire Department
Department of Health
Police Department
Department of Public Charities
Department of Parks, Manhattan and Richmond
Department of Parks, Brooklyn
Department of Parks, Bronx
Department of Parks, Queens
Department of Street Cleaning
Department of Water Supply, Gas and Electricity
Board of Assessors
Board of City Record
Board of Inebriety
Bureau of Weights and Measures
City Chamberlain
Municipal Civil Service Commission
Commissioners of Accounts
Department of Licenses
Department of Taxes and Assessments
Examining Board of Plumbers
Law Department
Mayor's Office
Public Recreation Commission
Tenement House Department

CO-OPERATIVE CENTRALIZED PURCHASING IN THE CITY OF NEW YORK

SUMMARY OF REPORT

Work Accomplished Through the Central Purchasing Committee and Resulting Benefits to the City

1 The mayor's central purchasing committee, organized November, 1914, has inaugurated a new consolidated contract procedure for the city, and with existing staffs has organized and equipped a central purchasing department to operate the plan. It has already consolidated practically all the contract purchasing of the twenty-eight departments and offices under the direct supervision of the mayor, which involves an expenditure of approximately $6,000,000 yearly.

2 The co-operative purchase plan obtains the benefits of central purchasing by consolidating into single contracts through voluntary arrangement the like requirements of 28 departments under the mayor, hitherto making their purchases independently. Only four of the committee's proposals were for individual departments. Ten, twelve and fourteen departments, respectively, joined in the proposals for cleaning material, forage and fuel.

3 The committee has prepared plans for consolidating open market orders, installing a central clearing house for the better utilization of department overstock and obsolete stores, and establishing central control over the departmental sale of condemned supplies, etc. The plan for the consolidation of open market orders has now been partially installed.

4 Fifty-five contract proposals for over thirty-five different classes of supplies have been advertised and 2,148 individual proposals have been given out to manufacturers, dealers, etc. The committee has received 919 separate bids, and has executed 499 joint contracts and open market order agreements.

5 Nine of the proposals advertised through the committee exceeded $100,000 in value—one of them amounting to over $870,000. The total value of the supplies purchased through the committee during the year ($3,636,707.46,)

approximated 42 per cent. of the total appropriations and special revenue bonds (issued to September 30, 1915) allotted to the mayor's departments for supplies, material, etc., during 1915.

6 The quantity of supplies purchased through the committee assumed very large proportions, including among other items, 4,140,885 pounds of fresh beef, 357 tons of bread, 247 tons of butter, 269,199 gross tons of coal, 487,360 dozen eggs, 174,863 gallons of gasoline, 7,308 tons of hay, 8,642 tons of oats and 4,771,105 quarts of milk.

7 An associate purchasing committee composed of experienced purchasing experts selected from the various participating departments was appointed early in the year. This committee was organized into sub-committees, each one in charge of the preparation of a joint proposal for a specific class of supplies. The result of this consolidation of the best purchasing experience to be found in the city government has been a decrease in the cost of many items of supplies.

8 In the case of practically all of the items purchased by the departmental experts co-operating through the committee, the prices have been as good as or better than the departments felt they could have obtained otherwise. This result has been furthered by the consolidation of quantities and mailing lists, the securing of amendments to specifications, the bettering of delivery conditions and by a number of other points written into the various proposals which have made them more attractive to dealers while of advantage to the city.

9 The average cost of anthracite coal, buckwheat No. 3, was reduced from $2.667 per gross ton to $2.351 per gross ton; bituminous coal, run of mine, from $3.563 per gross ton to $3.136 per gross ton; coffee from $.168 per pound to $.139 per pound; gasoline from $.142 per gallon to $.099 per gallon; laundry soap from $.045 per pound to $.039 per pound.

10 The average competition on each contract proposal has been increased, owing to the consolidation of the departmental mailing lists of dealers, and the addition to these lists of the names of many dealers attracted to city business for the first time by the new method of purchasing instituted by the committee. In the case of coal the average competition was increased from seven bidders in the departments to thirty-five through the central committee; on canned goods and groceries the increase was from eight to twenty; on cleaning materials and compounds

from nine to thirty-five, and on clothing, drygoods and notions from ten to thirty-five.

11 The expense to the city of printing, advertising and distributing proposals has been largely reduced. In the case of fuel, 14 departmental proposals were combined in one. The 55 proposals advertised through the committee were the equivalent of 173 individual departmental proposals.

12 The cost to the city of preparing and executing contracts has been materially reduced. The 499 contracts and open market order agreements executed through the committee were the equivalent of 1,149 individual departmental contracts and open market order agreements.

13 A material saving has resulted from a reduction of work in the board of city record, law department, bureau of standards—supply division, finance department, and in the individual participating departments, through the consolidation of proposals, contracts and all of the various papers connected therewith in the central purchasing committee.

14 Close contact with departments and dealers in the act of purchase has enabled the committee to recommend many beneficial changes in existing standards, while co-operation between the central purchasing committee and the bureau of standards has afforded the latter a favorable opportunity to test the merits of many tentative specifications not yet adopted.

15 The consolidation of departmental estimates for the various classes of supplies has enabled the committee to standardize articles, containers, samples and delivery conditions in many cases where these items had not already been covered by the bureau of standards.

16 The foundation has been firmly established for extending and developing the work during 1916 to cover the purchases of many more departments. Estimates of contract needs for 1916 have already been requested from the mayor's departments, a detailed plan prepared involving the immediate establishment of a central purchasing department on a permanent basis, and the assumption on January 1, 1916, of all the purchasing for four of the largest departments in the city government.

17 A central sample room has been established for the convenience of bidders, and they now realize that by coming to one place they can obtain the information formerly to be received only from a number of different sources. All complaints and requests for information have been given careful and courteous attention. Difficulties with inspec-

tion and delays in the payment of claims have been promptly adjusted. Every effort has been made by the central purchasing committee to make manufacturers and dealers feel that city business is good business and well worth their serious consideration.

Constructive Recommendations for Eliminating Defects in the Present Purchasing System

1 There should be a Board of City Purchase composed of five members. The mayor, the comptroller, one other member of the board of estimate and apportionment chosen by that body as a whole, and two representatives appointed by the mayor.

2 The purchasing function of the present board of city record should be transferred to the board of city purchase as soon as practicable.

3 The administrative head in direct charge of the work of central purchasing should be appointed by the chairman of the board or by the board as a whole.

4 The plan for the centralization of purchasing should be developed first among the mayor's departments, the other departments to participate at a later period either voluntarily or by order of the board of estimate and apportionment.

5 The board should undertake **all** purchasing for Bellevue and allied hospitals and the departments of health, public charities and correction on January 1, 1916, in addition to the present program of consolidated contract purchasing for the other mayor's departments. The entire purchasing of the other departments should be assumed by the board at later periods throughout the year as the development of its work will permit.

6 Proper provision should be made to enable the individual departments to continue to make emergency purchases.

7 Such part of the purchasing staffs of Bellevue and allied hospitals and the departments of health, public charities and correction as may be required should be transferred to the board of city purchase, as soon as the purchasing for the former departments has been consolidated. Those not transferred should be assigned to other work or discontinued, as in the case of the central payroll consolidation.

8 It is assumed that the purchasing experts transferred from the departments would be assigned by the board as assistant purchasing agents and specialists of the par-

ticular classes of supplies with whose purchase they are most experienced.

9 A central clearing house should be established as a part of the organization of the board, charged with the transfer of the inactive stores in the various departments to the departments needing them, and with central control over departmental sales of condemned supplies.

10 To remedy the present duplication and lack of uniformity of inspection, individual departmental inspection should be abolished and all supply inspection should be centered in the finance department.

11 There should be the closest co-operation between the board of city purchase and the bureau of standards, so that each organization could have the benefit of the knowledge and experience of the other. This is essential to economical purchasing and the establishment of effective supply standards.

12 Sufficient funds should be appropriated to place the work of the board of city purchase upon a permanent basis. $16,500 will be required to operate the office and to employ assistance in addition to that obtained from the present purchasing staffs of the individual departments.

13 A central supply fund should be established with specific sums allotted to the various departments to finance the purchase of supplies, etc., needed by each.

14 The board should be organized in three divisions, namely executive, administrative and operative. The operative functions should be: (a) Preparation, promotion and execution of consolidated contracts and open market orders; (b) transfer or sale of inactive departmental stores; and (c) accounting. The duties under the latter function should include the maintenance of price and statistical records and the general accounts of the board.

15 All estimates for contracts and requisitions for open market orders should continue to be prepared in the individual departments, the preparation, award and execution of contracts and open market orders being assumed by the board of city purchase.

16 Laws and ordinances should at once be prepared to permit the adoption of any constructive suggestions which it may now be impossible to carry out on account of legal restrictions.

17 Until proper legal provision has been made to permit the installation of the most effective plan of centralized city purchasing, the work begun during the past year should be continued.

ONE YEAR OF CO-OPERATIVE PURCHASING

How Work Was Done

The city has no central purchasing department. Nearly 100 separate departments are authorized to make purchases. The greater part of these purchases are made by departments under the control of the mayor. For these it was determined to obtain some of the advantages of central purchasing by combining demands into single proposals. To accomplish this the departments were obliged to work through a common agency. The committee has served as this agency. The mere physical problem of effecting co-operation between 28 different departments, each authorized by law and accustomed to act independently has in itself demanded great energy and tact. Without the co-operation of the commissioners, of course, the merging of individual interest and prerogative into the common cause would not have been possible. It is clear that all the advantages of central purchasing cannot be obtained without the actual establishment of one agency legally authorized to make all purchases, responsible for vouchering claims so that prompt settlement may be made with the consequent effect on prices, etc. But the test made, though necessarily incomplete, has demonstrated the plain sense and financial advantage of substituting one purchasing agency for a hundred.

Prompt Advertisement of First Contract Proposal

Within one month after the appointment of the committee, its first consolidated contract including four departments was actually advertised. The work was begun so late in the fall of 1914 that it was thought wise to attempt only the contract purchase of meat and poultry for the first quarter of 1915, and on the basis of this proposal, with the assistance of the law and finance departments, a consolidated contract procedure for the mayor's departments was worked out and adopted for the first time.

Development of Organization and System

As the volume of work undertaken by the committee has increased during the year, frequent changes have had to be made in the form of organization of the staff and in the method of procedure, until the present organization and procedure were finally evolved. These changes had to be made to meet new conditions without in any way retarding or interfering with the current contracting obligations assumed by the committee.

Rapid Increase in Work Undertaken

With the aid of the purchasing experts in the departments, consolidated contracts for practically all lines of food, with the addition of fuel and forage, were prepared and awarded during the second quarter of the year. These classes together with the completed line of supplies, material and equipment were purchased on contract through the committee for the second half of the year. Three of these contracts included ten, twelve and fourteen departments, respectively. In special cases with the consent of the committee the departments advertised contracts individually, but at the present time the committee is planning the preparation of all supplies, material and equipment contracts for the mayor's departments during 1916.

Approximately Forty-two Per Cent. of Departmental Purchases for 1915 Made Through Committee

Some idea of the volume of work accomplished through the committee may be gained from the fact that the total amount of cooperative purchases for the year was $3,636,707.46. This sum is 41.8 per cent. of the total appropriations and special revenue bonds (to September 30th) for supplies, material and equipment for the mayor's departments for 1915, less coal purchased in advance for 1916. The total volume of business transacted through the committee by the various departments compared with the total appropriations and special revenue bonds (to September 30th) for supplies, etc., granted to each department in 1915 is shown in the following tables:

TOTAL VOLUME OF BUSINESS TRANSACTED COMPARED WITH TOTAL APPROPRIATIONS AND SPECIAL REVENUE BONDS (SEPTEMBER 30TH) FOR SUPPLIES, ETC.

NAME OF DEPARTMENT, OFFICE, ETC.	Total Departmental Appropriations and Special Revenue Bonds (to Sept. 30, 1915) for Supplies, Material and Equipment During 1915	Total Amount Purchased Through the Central Purchasing Committee During 1915
*Armory Board	$45,340.00	$17,494.28
Bellevue and Allied Hospitals	704,604.00	425,441.05
Board of Assessors	184.50	....
Board of City Record	1,089.20	....
Board of Inebriety	7,487.00	94.50
Bureau of Weights and Measures	2,905.00	....
City Chamberlain	1,805.00	....
Commissioner of Accounts	3,724.07	....
Department of Bridges	90,524.79	10,534.20
Department of Public Charities	2,242,123.82	1,316,792.48
Department of Correction	687,257.28	291,094.70
Department of Docks and Ferries	365,610.72	4,411.55
Department of Health	694,123.76	379,458.68
Department of Licenses	11,033.00	....
Department of Parks, Manhattan and Richmond	128,664.25	15,365.64
Department of Parks, Brooklyn	82,956.34	15,996.51
Department of Parks, Queens	12,479.82	5,585.38
Department of Parks, Bronx	62,701.91	18,316.75
Department of Street Cleaning	979,578.94	488,084.32
Department of Taxes and Assessments	4,135.50	....
Department of Water Supply, Gas and Electricity	713,138.00	359,749.62
Examining Board of Plumbers	113.00	....
Fire Department	527,383.96	205,983.71
Law Department	7,100.00	....
Mayor's Office	1,300.00	....
Municipal Civil Service Commission	9,500.00	363.60
Police Department	241,093.17	81,688.15
Public Recreation Commission	715.00	....
Tenement House Department	10,330.20	152.34
Total	$7,639,002.23	†$3,636,707.46

* Co-operated with the Central Purchasing Committee on the fuel contract, though not one of the mayor's departments.

† Includes coal for the first quarter of 1916, valued at $441,254.94.

VALUE OF 1915 PURCHASES ON CONSOLIDATED CONTRACTS THROUGH THE CENTRAL PURCHASING COMMITTEE IN TOTAL AND BY INDIVIDUAL DEPARTMENTS.

No. of Proposals	Trade Classification	Total Value of Contracts	Bellevue and Allied Hospitals	Department of Public Charities	Department of Correction	Department of Health	Board of Inebriety	Department of Street Cleaning	Fire Department	Police Department	Department of Bridges	Department of Parks Manhattan and Richmond	Department of Parks, Brooklyn	Department of Parks, Queens	Department of Parks, Bronx	Department of Water Supply, Gas and Electricity	Armory Board	Tenement House Department	Department of Docks and Ferries	Municipal Civil Service Commission
8	Meats and Poultry	$873,239.03	$137,496.23	$466,246.25	$164,981.16	$104,515.39														
2	Coffee	41,492.14	4,412.64	22,561.60	10,837.40	3,586.00	$94.50													
2	Milk and Cream	269,335.25	40,441.78	161,216.44	28,365.84	39,311.19														
6	Fruits and Vegetables	103,448.44	13,455.47	63,370.57	13,901.63	12,720.77														
4	Butter, Cheese, Eggs, Bread, Rolls	271,146.45	55,665.03	167,831.94	3,974.55	43,674.93														
3	Canned Goods and Groceries	153,063.70	24,433.16	93,579.54	13,921.45	21,129.55														
1	Fish, Clams, etc.	14,217.28	9,668.60			4,548.68														
2	Forage	645,257.75		5,985.93	4,746.60	17,766.54		$479,736.70	$87,186.02	$34,309.67	$1,036.05	$5,273.65	$6,040.02	$929.33	$491.10	$1,756.14				
4	Coal, Gasoline, Cordwood	996,769.50	91,498.63	279,283.78	47,835.31	53,408.79		7,037.71	82,634.16	43,771.85	3,518.44	9,230.12	8,248.75	4,656.05	16,600.12	331,551.51	$17,494.28			
2	Drugs, Chemicals, Reagents	73,808.48	1,387.50	23,460.61		29,032.84		1,309.91	610.42							18,007.20				
1	Lubricants and Kerosene	6,249.17	433.73	477.38	174.75				2,022.57	844.24						1,771.50			$525.00	
2	Cleaning Materials, etc.	24,160.52	3,965.41	9,796.74	183.36	3,335.01			4,238.02	1,985.21		403.58	53.08		7.73	192.38				
2	Photographic Supplies, etc.	3,132.15	1,641.52	1,338.29														$152.34		
2	Paints, Oils, Varnishes, etc.	10,700.90	1,419.04		313.80	2,541.83			4,241.81	465.64						233.28			1,485.50	
1	Cement, Lime, Sand, etc.	2,735.36		875.26					161.85		1,410.00					159.25			129.00	
1	Cordage, Rope, Oakum	3,040.44	123.17	830.26	148.00				1,135.88		208.93					222.15			372.05	
1	Flowering Bulbs	3,330.75										458.29	1,654.66		1,217.80					
1	Auto Chains, Tires, etc.	4,851.84							4,851.84											
2	Laboratory Apparatus, etc.	77,271.33	31,208.23	13,984.38		32,078.72														
2	Lumber	12,341.86	717.93	5,713.75					2,567.39		2,787.00					555.79				
1	Iron, Steel, and Other Metals	7,500.00	135.66	239.76	188.00				2,006.62		1,573.78					1,456.18			1,900.00	
1	Pipe, Pipe Fittings, etc.	17,841.00	2,960.46		77.50				12,217.23							2,585.81				
1	Furniture and Furnishings	1,130.14			60.00				395.00	311.54										$363.60
2	Household Wares	4,929.64	275.11			4,654.53														
1	Clothing, Dry Goods, etc.	15,714.34	4,101.75		1,485.35	7,153.91			1,714.90							1,258.43				
55		$3,636,707.46	$425,441.05	$1,316,792.48	$291,194.70	$379,458.68	$94.50	$488,084.32	$205,983.71	$81,688.15	$10,534.20	$15,365.64	$15,996.51	$5,585.38	$18,316.75	$359,749.62	$17,494.28	$152.34	$4,411.55	$363.60

499 Joint Contracts, etc., Executed

During the year fifty-five joint contract proposals were advertised through the committee involving thirty-five classes of supplies. In nine of the proposals the value in each case exceeded $100,000.00, one of them amounting to over $870,000.00. 2,148 proposals were given out to individual manufacturers and dealers, which meant personal interviews in the offices of the committee in over seventy-five per cent. of the cases. 919 separate bids were submitted at the various bid openings, and 499 joint contracts and open market order agreements were executed, as shown in the accompanying schedule:

Quantity of Supplies, Materials and Equipment Purchased

A better realization of the vast quantities of food, forage, etc., purchased for the city in 1915 through this committee may be obtained from the following statement of the total quantity of a number of items most commonly used:

Name of Article	Number of Depts. Participating	Period Covered	Total Quantity Purchased
		Months	
Beans, white	4	9	125,920 lbs.
Beef, fresh	4	12	4,140,885 lbs.
Bread	3	9	715,493 lbs.
Butter	4	9	494,130 lbs.
Cheese Cloth	3	6	424,100 yds.
Chloride of Lime	1	6	1,204,000 lbs.
Coal	14	12	269,199 gr. tons
Coffee	4	11	365,100 lbs.
Cornmeal	4	9	80,640 lbs.
Cotton, absorbent	2	6	18,350 lbs.
Eggs	4	9	487,360 doz.
Farina	4	9	76,860 lbs.
Flowering Bulbs	3	6	460,500 single bulbs
Gasoline	10	6	174,863 gals.
Gauze, plain absorbent	2	6	1,133,000 yds.
Ham	4	12	171,535 lbs.
Hay	12	9	14,617,355 lbs.
Macaroni	4	9	60,500 lbs.
Milk, pasteurized	4	9	4,771,105 qts.
Mutton	4	12	1,137,765 lbs.
Oatmeal	4	9	198,510 lbs.
Oats	12	9	17,284,430 lbs.
Peas, dried	4	9	51,620 lbs.
Potatoes, white	4	9	4,620,811 lbs.
Prunes	4	9	176,925 lbs.
Salt, table	4	9	317,960 lbs.
Soap, laundry	7	6	195,008 lbs.
Sugar, granulated	4	9	971,468 lbs.
White Lead	6	6	113,000 lbs.

ADVANTAGES DERIVED BY THE CITY FROM CO-OPERATIVE PURCHASING

The work of co-operative buying, so far undertaken through a central agency, despite the drawbacks of inadequate and defective legal provisions compelling delays in the execution of contracts and annoyance to commissioners through the multiplicity of documentary signatures, has been of sufficient success and has produced sufficient economies to warrant its continuance until corrective legislation may be passed.

Summary of Advantages

The following is a summary of the advantages derived by the city from co-operative buying during the current year:

1 As a result of the consolidation of purchases, the cost of supplies has been decreased.

2 Competition has been widened by the addition of many new bidders and the use of a consolidated mailing list.

3 Additional standards have been established for supplies and materials and old standards revised, thereby reducing the cost of beef, mutton, ham, coffee, etc., and removing uncertainty of the meaning of proposals.

4 There has been a marked reduction in the cost and labor of preparing proposals and contracts.

5 The central purchasing committee has proven itself an aid to manufacturers, dealers, etc., in conducting their business with the city on a businesslike and direct basis, thereby inviting increased competition.

6 The central purchasing committee has functioned as a bureau of information and complaints.

7 Larger quantities, fewer delivery points, smaller territory within which deliveries are to be made and short term contracts have made proposals more attractive to the trade.

8 The establishment of a central sample room has been a great convenience to bidders.

9 The centralization of purchases has reduced the work of other central agencies of the city government.

Advantages in Detail

Decreased Prices

Any advantage in price obtained through the committee can be no reflection on the past work of the department's purchasing agents,

STATISTICAL DATA RELATING TO THE VARIOUS JOINT PROPOSALS ADVERTISED THROUGH THE CENTRAL PURCHASING COMMITTEE

No. of Proposal	Date of Opening	Trade Classification	Period Covered During 1915		Proposals Issued	Bids Received	Contracts and O. M. O. Awarded			Value of Awards
			From	To			Contracts	Orders	Total	
1	Dec. 24, 1914	Meats and Poultry	Jan. 1	Mar. 31	33	10	9	..	9	$219,068.49
2	Feb. 5, 1915	Coffee—Green Santos	Feb. 1	Dec. 31	43	10	1	..	1	30,733.50
3	Feb. 23, 1915	Coffee—Green Bogota	Feb. 1	Dec. 31	24	4	1	..	1	10,758.64
4	Mar. 15, 1915	Meats and Poultry	April 1	April 30	35	15	7	2	9	70,088.86
5	Mar. 29, 1915	Milk and Cream	April 1	Sept. 30	14	9	3	2	5	160,560.41
6	Mar. 29, 1915	Fruits and Vegetables	April 1	June 30	20	6	Bids Rejected			....
7	Mar. 29, 1915	Butter, Cheese, Eggs, Bread and Rolls	April 1	June 30	41	19	4	1	5	85,521.42
8	Mar. 30, 1915	Forage	Mar. 31	June 30	34	15	7	..	7	208,215.95
9	Mar. 31, 1915	Canned Goods and Groceries	April 1	June 30	42	21	8	9	17	57,609.89
10	Mar. 31, 1915	Fuel—Coal	April 1	June 30	51	30	13	3	16	114,999.40
11	April 12, 1915	Stock Fruits and Vegetables	April 13	May 31	19	7	4	1	5	18,068.47
12	April 15, 1915	Fish, Oysters, Clams, etc	April 1	Dec. 31	12	4	2	..	2	14,217.28
13	April 15, 1915	Meats and Poultry	May 1	May 31	32	19	6	7	13	60,293.87
14	April 28, 1915	Meats and Poultry	May 1	May 31	16	6	3	1	4	13,885.46
15	May 14, 1915	Stock Fruits and Vegetables	June 1	June 30	13	7	2	2	4	15,739.72
16	May 14, 1915	Meats and Poultry	June 1	June 30	21	14	7	5	12	76,779.08
17	May 20, 1915	Coal, Gasoline and Cordwood	July 1	Mar. 31 ('16)	82	42	Bids Rejected			....
18	June 4, 1915	Meats and Poultry	July 1	July 31	33	11	9	0	9	79,302.91
19	June 4, 1915	Butter, Cheese, Eggs, Bread and Rolls	July 1	Sept. 30	27	7	2	0	2	45,089.98
20	June 4, 1915	Stock Fruits and Vegetables	July 1	Sept. 30	13	8	4	0	4	24,218.27
21	June 11, 1915	Fuel—Coal, Gasoline, Cordwood	July 1	Mar. 31 ('16)	77	40	24	2	26	873,700.10
22	June 11, 1915	Forage	July 1	Dec. 31	35	13	8	0	8	437,041.80
23	June 18, 1915	Butter, Cheese, Eggs, etc	July 1	Sept. 30	44	5	4	0	4	75,153.55
24	June 18, 1915	Canned Goods and Groceries	July 1	Sept. 30	35	21	9	6	15	55,514.53
25	June 18, 1915	Lubricants and Kerosene	July 1	Dec. 31	45	16	3	6	9	6,249.17
26	June 30, 1915	Cleaning Materials, etc	July 1	Dec. 31	110	40	Bids Not Opened			....
27	June 30, 1915	Drugs, Chemicals, etc	July 1	Dec. 31	67	27	10	7	17	53,293.68
28	June 30, 1915	Photographic Supplies	July 1	Dec. 31	21	7	Bids Rejected			....
29	June 30, 1915	White Potatoes	July 1	Sept. 30	12	10	1	1	2	14,421:39
30	July 7, 1915	Paints, Oils, Varnishes	July 10	Dec. 31	68	16	3	5	8	8,605.08
31	July 7, 1915	Cement, Lime, Sand, etc	July 10	Dec. 31	32	15	1	8	9	2,735.36
32	July 7, 1915	Cordage, Rope and Oakum	July 10	Dec. 31	25	7	1	4	5	3,040.44
33	July 7, 1915	Lumber, etc	July 10	Dec. 31	35	9	2	1	3	9,695.98
34	July 8, 1915	Flowering Bulbs	July 10	Dec. 15	14	6	1	1	2	3,330.75
35	July 12, 1915	Auto Chains, Tires, etc	July 15	Dec. 31	34	9	3	1	4	4,851.84
36	July 19, 1915	Meats and Poultry	Aug. 1	Sept. 30	12	11	9	0	9	160,599.77
37	July 21, 1915	Cleaning Materials	Aug. 1	Dec. 31	56	35	8	12	20	24,160.52
38	July 27, 1915	Drugs, Chemicals, etc	Aug. 1	Dec. 31	44	19	5	7	12	20,514.80
39	July 27, 1915	Laboratory Apparatus	Aug. 1	Dec. 31	115	66	17	27	44	69,215.68
40	July 27, 1915	Lumber	Aug. 1	Dec. 31	22	6	1	3	4	2,645.88
41	Aug. 6, 1915	Iron, Steel and Other Metals	Sept. 1	Dec. 31	30	18	4	7	11	7,500.00
42	Aug. 6, 1915	Paints, Oils, Varnishes, etc	Sept. 1	Dec. 31	19	10	1	5	6	2,095.82
43	Aug. 6, 1915	Laboratory Apparatus, etc	Sept. 1	Dec. 31	45	28	4	16	20	8,055.65
44	Aug. 23, 1915	Furniture and Furnishings	Sept. 1	Dec. 31	57	20	0	8	8	1,130.14
45	Aug. 23, 1915	Photographic Supplies	Sept. 1	Dec. 31	14	4	2	1	3	3,132.15
46	Aug. 27, 1915	Pipe, Pipe Fittings, etc	Oct. 1	Dec. 31	218	78	9	40	49	17,841.00
47	Aug. 27, 1915	Household Ware	Sept. 1	Dec. 31	41	13	2	3	5	3,252.85
48	Aug. 27, 1915	Clothing, Dry Goods, etc	Sept. 1	Dec. 31	93	35	8	17	25	15,714.34
49	Sept. 17, 1915	Meats and Poultry	Oct. 1	Dec. 31	18	14	10	1	11	193,220.59
50	Sept. 17, 1915	Fruits and Vegetables	Oct. 1	Dec. 31	12	6	3	2	5	31,000.59
51	Sept. 17, 1915	Coal	Oct. 1	Oct. 31	11	4	1	0	1	8,070.00
52	Sept. 24, 1915	Butter, Cheese, Eggs, etc	Oct. 1	Dec. 31	29	10	5	3	8	65,381.50
53	Sept. 24, 1915	Milk and Cream	Oct. 1	Dec. 31	10	8	4	0	4	108,774.84
54	Oct. 1, 1915	Canned Goods and Groceries	Oct. 1	Dec. 31	41	23	8	9	17	39,939.28
55	Oct. 1, 1915	Household Ware	Oct. 1	Dec. 31	12	6	1	0	1	1,676.79
					2,148	919	264	235	499	$3,636,707.46

for to them is due in large measure the success of the committee's work by reason of their active and continuous co-operation with and participation in the committee's work.

In making every award the departments have investigated the price of each item with great care, and in practically every case where the co-operative price in their opinion could be bettered in the open market or by readvertising, they have rejected the bid. As a result, practically the entire amount purchased through the committee represents prices which are as good or better than the departments felt at the time they could otherwise obtain.

The European war with the consequent decrease in our imports and increase in exports has had such an effect on practically every class of items purchased through the committee, that it is difficult to make any reliable comparison of prices between 1915 and 1914. The cost of innumerable items has been raised in this city by decreased supply due to the above causes. In the case of some classes local conditions have assisted in affecting the price. This is particularly true of forage, flour and fresh meat. In consequence, many co-operative prices accepted by the departments while exceptionally low in view of the market conditions in 1915 are high in comparison with 1914 prices. There are some items easily obtainable in 1914 which now cannot be purchased at all.

In departments with exceptionally well organized and equipped purchasing divisions, the co-operative prices have about held their own, but on averaging the co-operative prices obtained by all the participating departments the result is one of the strong arguments for the continuance of central purchasing. In every case where the associate committee, composed of the department purchasing experts, has been able to study intensively the consolidated proposals to be advertised for the supply class placed in its charge, the price results have been most satisfactory. The prices obtained for food and fuel are examples of the effect of this type of co-operation. As each succeeding class proposal prepared by the various sub-committees must show more and more the effect of their united experience, and as the sub-committees make every endeavor to correct the defects developed in their previous proposals, the beneficial results obtained from the consolidated proposals advertised in 1916 should materially exceed those of this year.

Although purchases by the departments individually and those through the central purchasing committee were rarely if ever made under the same conditions, an attempt has been made in the following table to select a few items in most common use and least affected by the changed market conditions in 1915, as a basis of comparison of the average price obtained through the central committee in 1915 with the average price obtained by the co-operating departments individually in 1914:

Statement Showing Comparison of Average Price Obtained in 1915 Through the Central Purchasing Committee with the Average Price Obtained in 1914 by the Mayor's Departments Individually on Various Items in Common Use and Least Effected by Changed Market Conditions.

Name of Article	Unit of Quantity	Average Price Secured by Departments in 1914	Average Price Secured through Central Purch. Committee in 1915	Total Quantity Purchased in 1915 through Central Purch. Committee
Anthractite Coal, Nut	Gross Ton	6.571	6.544	1,723
Anthracite Coal, Buckwheat No. 3	Gross Ton	2.667	2.351	36,175
Bituminous Coal, Run of Mine	Gross Ton	3.536	3.136	60,710
Bacon	Pound	.171	.1606	89,015
Baking Powder	*Pound	.2133	.1923	3,293
Butter	*Pound	.2823	.2659	494,130
Canned Apricots, No. 10 tins	*Dozen	6.285	5.50	68
Canned Corn, No. 10 tins	*Dozen	6.00	5.22	95
Canned Tomatoes, No. 10 tins	*Dozen	2.68	2.12	686
Cheese Cloth	†Yard	.028	.0223	133,100
Chloride of Lime in drums	†Pound	.01333	.0118	1,204,000
Chickens	Pound	.1943	.1877	224,760
Coffee	Pound	.16794	.13944	365,100
Cotton, Absorbent, 1 lb. packages	†Pound	.1894	.17	18,350
Eggs, Candled	*Dozen	.2481	.232	161,360
Flannel, Outing	†Yard	.0635	.0547	4,250
Gauze, plain absorbent, in bales of 2,400 yards	†Yard	.02035	.01775	1,133,000
Gasoline	†Gallon	.1419	.0995	174,863
Hams, Smoked	Pound	.1617	.1484	171,535
Laundry Soap	†Pound	.04473	.039	195,008
Lard	*Pound	.12198	.1033	7,040
Linseed Oil, boiled	†Gallon	.71	.65	1,130
Milk	*Quart	.05829	.05315	4,771,105
Prunes, 50 lb. boxes	*Pound	.10375	.0818	166,900
Potatoes, white	*Pound	.0133	.01214	4,602,811
Rice	*Pound	.0524	.0493	72,950
Rubber Coats	†Each	2.507	1.90	100
Salt, Table, 280 lb. bbls.	*Pound	.005935	.005885	87,400
Spruce, Studs, 2" x 4" x 16' long	†M.ft.B.M.	29.00	27.00	2,665 ft. B. M.
Towels, Bleached, Turkish, Bath	†Dozen	3.52	2.20	146
Turpentine	†Gallon	.4783	.4245	3,800
Uniforms, Nurses, White Drill	†Suit	1.13	.025	884
Vinegar	*Gallon	.1399	.11	5,069
White Pine, 1" x 12" x 12' and up, D 2/s to 7/8"	†M.ft.B.M.	83.00	79.00	2,000 ft. B. M.

* The comparison here is between 1914 entire and the last 9 months of 1915.

† The comparison here is between 1914 entire and the last 6 months of 1915.

Competition for Contracts has been Widened

The combined effort of the several departments in advertising consolidated contracts has resulted in wider competition on the majority of the proposals issued by the central purchasing committee than was previously secured by the individual departments on proposals covering the same classes of goods. The departmental representatives have furnished the central committee with extensive lists of dealers, and have personally assisted in bringing the various proposals to the attention of the manufacturers, etc., with whom they had previously traded. A large number of firms have made a direct request of the committee to be placed upon its mailing list, with the result that many bids have been received during the year from dealers who had never bid on city business before, or who for some reason had previously withdrawn their competition. This increased competition, with the impression it has made on old bidders, has materially assisted the co-operating departments in obtaining favorable prices.

CHART SHOWING~COMPARISON OF AVERAGE NUMBER OF BIDS RECEIVED BY THE CENTRAL PURCHASING COMMITTEE IN 1915, AND BY THE INDIVIDUAL DEPARTMENTS IN 1914.

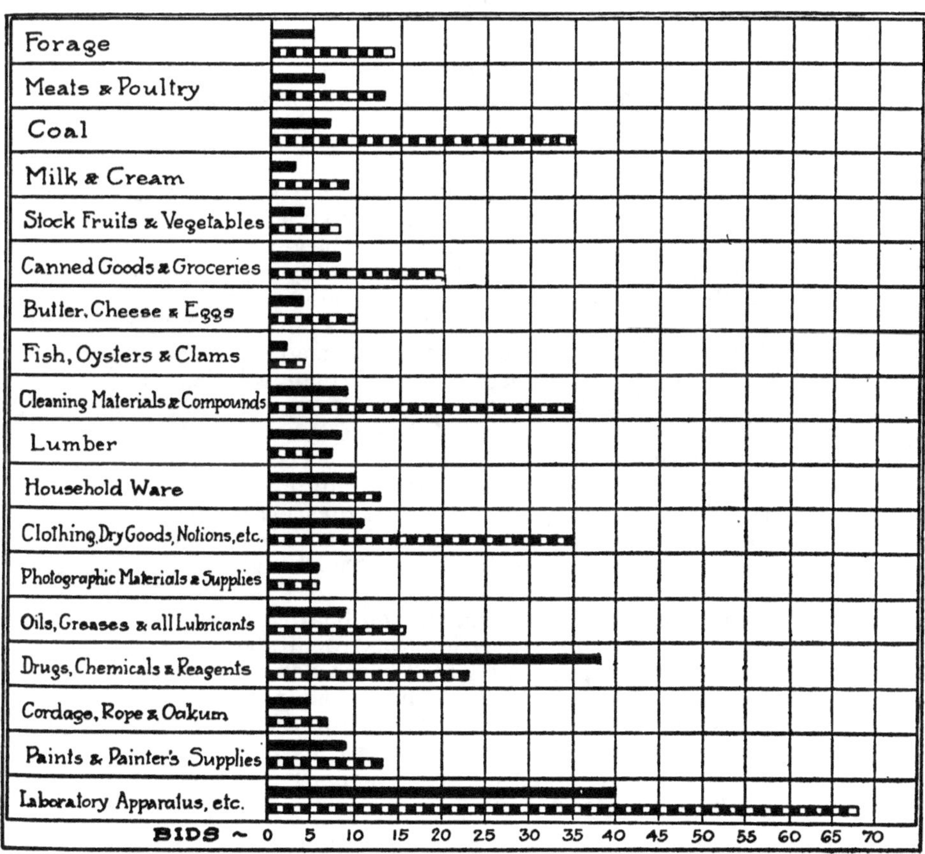

~ EXPLANATORY ~

Individual Department - - - - shown thus

Central Purchasing Committee ~ ~ shown thus

The above chart indicates the average competition received by the central purchasing committee on its consolidated proposals during 1915 compared with that received by the individual departments during 1914 on proposals covering the same classes of articles.

Additional Standards Established for Supplies and Material, and Old Standards Revised

Obviously, central purchasing offers opportunities for standardization not existing under decentralized purchasing. Bringing into one schedule the requirements of the departments in particular lines demonstrates plainly the need of agreement upon common specifications or samples and the economy to be derived from each department using the same thing for the same purpose. Furthermore, centralization of purchasing by reason of concentration of experience, brings out more distinctly than decentralization the defects in existing standard specifications which tend to prevent the widest possible competition.

The following are a few instances when, by the aid of the committee, purchasing has been made more effective and economical:

1 *Changes in Meat and Poultry Specifications*

The first contract of the central purchasing committee—that for meats and poultry—brought out plainly the need of revising the specifications covering these articles. The specifications under which meat and poultry for the first quarter of the year were purchased excluded frozen mutton, and were interpreted by several dealers also to exclude chilled Argentine beef, both being cheaper grades of meat, but quite as serviceable as those in use. To correct these and other defects information was secured from the department of agriculture of the United States government, and from other large users, including the army and navy, and the large hotels of New York City. In the light of this information the departments agreed upon suggestions which were submitted formally to the bureau of standards. A meeting was called by that bureau to discuss these suggestions, with the result that revised meat and poultry specifications were promulgated and adopted by the board of estimate and apportionment. This decision was facilitated by a dinner at one of the hospitals at which fresh domestic beef and mutton and chilled Argentine beef and frozen mutton were placed before a number of those interested in the test the majority of whom were unable to distinguish between the fresh and the chilled meats. Under these revised meat and poultry specifications:

a Chilled Argentine beef is expressly admitted to competition with native beef. The difference in price averages between one and two cents per pound, which meant on the amounts included in the contract for the first quarter's beef a saving of from $9,000 to $18,000.

b Frozen mutton is expressly admitted, which meant on the first quarter's contract, at a difference of about one and one-half cents per pound as against fresh mutton, a saving of about $5,400.

c The cut of pork loins was extended to include the regular commercial New York cut instead of confining it as before to the short cut, and the range of weights was widened.

d Specifications for fresh hams were changed to permit the delivery of good commercial quality instead of prime quality theretofore required. Weights were made more liberal and the permissible thickness of fat extended, resulting in reduced cost.

e Specifications for sausages were made more exacting and the requirement added that they be U. S. inspected and passed, thereby reducing the allowable percentage of cereal from five to two per cent.

f Specifications for bacon were changed to admit good commercial quality instead of confining deliveries to prime quality.

g Specifications for smoked hams were changed to admit good commercial quality instead of prime quality heretofore required. The range of weights was widened and the limitation of fat expanded.

h New specifications were prepared for bologna and frankfurter sausages, none existing for the latter article and a very inexact one for the former.

i Pork shoulders were to be good commercial quality instead of prime quality previously required, and the range of weights was widened.

j On all poultry, seasonal periods were introduced during which frozen poultry might be admitted. The weights of roosters and of chickens were widened, and it was plainly stated that receipts would be given for weights as received at points of delivery instead of at the several institutions, the latter provision in the former specifications being unfair to dealers, as it made them responsible for shrinkage in redistribution by the departments from points of delivery to points of use.

2 *Changes in Forage Specifications*

The specification for timothy hay was declared by dealers and departments to be very difficult to fulfill as it excluded all clover. At the suggestion of the representatives of the departments interested, the bureau of standards was requested by the central committee to change the specification for this article to admit clover among the other tame grasses which might be present in a bale of hay to the extent of not more than one-eighth of the entire bale.

It was further requested that the specification be changed to admit either large or small bales, whereas the previous specification required that large bales be delivered, unless the state of the market prohibited such deliveries. The bureau of standards after a conference on this subject acceded to the request. The change has operated very advantageously to the city.

3 *Standardization of Canned Goods and Groceries*

While no changes in the specifications for canned goods and groceries have been requested, by bringing together samples at one point opportunity has been offered for the elimination of unnecessary and expensive sizes of containers and for uniting upon one standard sample.

4 *Standardization of Motor Gasoline*

A specification for motor gasoline was agreed upon by nine departments, the specification adopted being the one which had proved most satisfactory to the department of water supply, gas and electricity. This specification was used in the committee's consolidated proposal for the latter half of the year, and resulted in obtaining an exceptionally low price.

5 *Standardization of Coffee*

Specifications were prepared by the committee after consultation with the trade, large consumers and the Produce Exchange, covering Santos and Bogota coffee, to be purchased green by the city and roasted for all departments by the department of public charities. Agreement upon these two brands of coffee supplanted eight brands, roasted and unroasted, bought during the previous year by the four institutional departments. Two-thirds of a more expensive grade formerly used was discarded for a cheaper grade, after those interested had tested both grades in the cup without being able to distinguish them. This reduction in grade saved the city over $5,000. The department of correction was also enabled to give its inmates a better coffee than they had had for a number of years at a material reduction in cost.

6 *Standardization of Lubricants*

While little opportunity was given for intensive work in standardizing the varied requirements of the several departments for lubricants, the central purchasing committee was able to secure the consent of two other departments to the common use of the specifications of the fire department for engine oil, and for cylinder, dynamo, and marine engine oil.

7 *Standardization of Cleaning Materials and Compounds*

Cleaning materials and compounds offered large opportunity for standardization of containers and of conditions of delivery. Many changes were made in reducing quarterly or monthly deliveries to single deliveries covering a longer period, and in securing uniformity of size of containers. For example, two departments agreed upon one sample for harness dressing, each formerly having a separate sample of different sized container. The four park departments agreed upon one kind of metal polish. Several departments agreed to accept soap powder in 350 pound barrels instead of in one pound cans. All departments agreed upon 80 pound cases of laundry soap, whereas formerly several departments had required cases of a different weight.

8 *Standardization of Drugs, Chemicals and Reagents*

Containers were standardized as far as the needs of the departments would permit, to allow of purchases in larger quantities in a single container.

9 *Standardization of Masons' Materials.*

A specification was agreed upon for Portland cement, the material for this specification being adapted from the specifitions of the American Society for Testing Materials, and the tentative specification of the bureau of standards. This specification met the approval of the engineers of all the departments interested in this contract.

10 *Standardization of Flowering Bulbs*

A standard specification for flowering bulbs was devised after consultation with the three park departments concerned in this contract.

11 *Standardization of Iron, Steel and other Metals.*

At the request of the department of water supply, gas and electricity, made through the central purchasing committee, a new standard specification for valve bronze castings was prepared by the bureau of standards.

The foregoing changes were taken advantage of by the committee in its various consolidated contract proposals. The first year's work has involved too much detail, incident to the working out of a new procedure for contract purchases, to permit a great amount of work of the above character to be done. Material is available, however, in the consolidated schedules of the central purchasing committee for greater intensive work in future standardization of various kinds. Recently, a meeting, at which representatives of large manufacturers were present, was held to discuss the specifications and form of proposal for cleaning materials and compounds. Several suggestions were secured at this meeting which, if put into effect, should extend competition in these commodities. In interviews held since this meeting with the representatives of manufacturers who were unwilling to express their views at a public conference, many more valuable suggestions have been secured. Through such conferences and interviews with the trade, and by continuing study of the requirements of the departments, complete and effective standardization may shortly be secured through the operation of central purchasing.

Reduction in Cost of Preparing and Issuing Proposals

There are many elements of cost to the city in the production of a contract proposal, including preparation, promotion and execution, and the cost of advertising, printing, etc. Based on the extent of participation in the committee's joint proposals by the various departments, under the individual purchasing plan these departments would have had to prepare and advertise 173 contract proposals as compared with the 51 which were actually awarded through the committee. For example, in the committee's fuel proposal covering the nine months beginning July 1, 1915, fourteen separate departmental proposals were combined in one. Of the 51 proposals advertised by the committee only four were for single departments. Without attempting to reduce the comparative cost of consolidated and individual departmental proposals to dollars and cents, it is clearly evident that consolidation has resulted in a material saving to the city in money and labor.

Reduction in Cost of Preparing and Issuing Contracts

The same is true with regard to contracts. In the case of the consolidated coal proposal cited above, 25 joint contracts were executed in which were consolidated 73 departmental contracts and 44 departmental open market order agreements. In other words, the 25 joint contracts took the place of 117 departmental contracts and open market order agreements which would have been required under the former system. The 499 joint contracts and open market order agreements executed through the committee were the actual equivalent of 1149 individual departmental contracts, etc.

Central Purchasing Committee an Aid to Dealers

An effort has been made in the preparation of each of the 55 proposals advertised through the central purchasing committee during the present year to make business with the city attractive to dealers and thereby widen competition. In the various trade classes this effort has taken different directions. In proposals covering some classes of articles greater progress has been made than in others towards securing what the central purchasing committee and its associated members consider the most attractive form consistent with the protection of the city's interest. In general it may be stated that from interviews with dealers, many hundreds of whom have received the committee's proposals during the past year, the business of the city has become more attractive to them through centralization by reason of the following facts:

1 Dealers prefer to come to one place for information regarding the city's requirements in place of the several necessitated by decentralization. Through centralization dealers know that all of the contract requirements of the mayor's departments may be brought to their attention at one interview and the danger avoided of losing sight of any part of them. It has been the rule for the staff of the committee to answer definitely, accurately and courteously the many requests for information that are continually being received from dealers. All complaints have been given careful attention, and the committee has functioned as a central bureau of information and complaints to a large number of dealers engaged in doing business with the city.

2 Consolidation of quantities in several of the proposals has made attractive to many dealers business which heretofore has offered no interest to them on account of the small quantities required. For example, the proposals for meats and poultry have contained the combined quantities for four departments for the city as a whole or by zones: the proposals for coffee, milk, butter, cheese and eggs, forage, coal, canned goods and groceries, stock fruits and vegetables, cleaning materials and compounds, drugs, chemicals and reagents and laboratory apparatus, surgical instruments, hospital and miscellaneous supplies, have been drawn in the same way with as many as fourteen departments combined in one proposal, and have offered the same opportunity. Dealers in several of these lines have expressed a high degree of satisfaction at this method of purchase and have stated expressly that the low prices offered by them have been due largely to this element.

3 An effort has been made to centralize samples in order to facilitate their inspection by dealers. Thus the samples for canned goods and groceries, cleaning materials and compounds, household ware, clothing, drygoods and notions, drugs, chemicals and reagents, and laboratory apparatus, surgical instruments, hospital and miscellaneous supplies for four or more departments have been consolidated and exhibited in one place. A sample room has been equipped with shelving and it is planned to take over as rapidly as possible the necessary samples for all proposals. Dealers have frequently stated that this is a great convenience to them.

4 In order that proposals might not contain consolidated quantities which were too large to admit of competition by dealers of medium capacity, quantities in several instances have been divided and offered in two or more lots. Thus, in the second contract for meat, the combined quantities of beef carcass for the borough of Manhattan, totaling 165,000 pounds, were divided into three lots of about 55,000 pounds each. Small dealers, who could not have handled the entire amount, have been able to bid upon one or more of these lots, whereas large dealers have in no way been restricted by such division.

5 Effort has been made to make the periods of the several contracts conform to the necessities of trade conditions. The

European war has introduced an element of instability into many lines, and dealers naturally have been cautious in binding themselves for periods so protracted as to make it impossible for them to forecast prices or the availability of their goods. The first contract for meat and poultry was for a period of three months. Consultation with dealers brought out the fact, however, that a number of them preferred an even shorter period during the spring and summer of this year, when fluctuations in prices were the greatest. Beginning with April, therefore, the contracts for meat and poultry were drawn for one month. In the case of the proposals for canned goods and groceries, the departments individually in 1914 had contracted for varying periods of six months to a year. It was agreed, however, by the members of the Associate Committee, after consultation with the trade, that a three months' contract in the class would produce better results under existing conditions.

6 Much care was taken in grouping the requirements of the departments to bring into the several proposals articles having a trade relationship so that dealers might more readily find classes of articles in which they were interested. For example, in the fuel proposal, anthracite and bituminous coal were offered separately. The former was divided into domestic, pea and buckwheat, and these in turn were divided into truck, carload and barge deliveries, giving an opportunity for bidding to mining companies as well as to wholesale and retail dealers.

7 In some instances the number of delivery points has been reduced and large immediate deliveries specified. On the proposal for coffee, covering the requirements of the four institutional departments from February to the end of the year, it was decided to ask for two deliveries of the 188 tons of coffee required, both to be made to one point—Blackwell's Island—to be roasted by the department of public charities and distributed in city boats already in operation to the several departmental institutions. Butter for two departments for the latter part of the year was purchased in July in bulk for immediate delivery to a storage warehouse. In both of these cases the purchase was made at a time when the market price was lowest.

The central purchasing committee has heard very little comment from dealers adverse to the new plan of centralization, but on the other hand has had numerous voluntary testimontials to the advantages which the dealers feel they are receiving through the change.

Cost of Printing and Advertising by Board of City Record Reduced

The board of city record is one of the central agencies of the city through which the purchasing divisions of all the city departments must do their contract advertising and printing. During the year it has assisted in every way in facilitating the work of the central committee. The benefits derived by the board from the inauguration of co-operative buying is outlined in the following letter recently received from its supervisor, Mr. David Ferguson:

"September 30th, 1915.

Central Purchasing Committee.

Sirs:

In the matter of relative cost of publishing advertisements for proposals in the CITY RECORD, and for printing contract proposals, specifications, etc., I beg to advise you that the centralization of the purchase of many supplies required by several of the departments in the Central Purchasing Committee, has lessened the expense to this office. One contract and one advertisement frequently represented what would have been four or five contracts and four or five separate advertisements. The saving is so obvious that little more need be said on that subject. In addition to the lessened money expense, centralization of this sort means less detail for this office to handle. It is clearly much easier to handle one advertisement for one central body than four or five separate advertisements from four or five different departments. The same is true of requisitions for printing contracts, etc., and shipping supplies from our distributing division.

Respectfully,

DAVID FERGUSON,
Supervisor of the City Record."

Work of Law Department Simplified

While the law department has given generously of its time in co-operating with the committee on the legal points involved in the adoption of a new consolidated contract procedure for the city, its routine work of examining and approving the form of each contract advertised heretofore by the individual departments has been greatly lessened and simplified through the present consolidation. The most striking illustration of this is in the consolidated fuel proposal advertised through the committee in June, 1915. In this case fourteen departments participated in advertising one joint proposal. Under the old system in place of the one proposal the law department would have had to examine and pass upon the forms of fourteen separate proposals, probably no two of which would have been prepared alike.

Using the same consolidated proposal as an example, the law department in all of the many legal matters which may arise with any contract, had to come in contact with only one central agency in place of fourteen departments, and to discuss and settle the legal points involved in only one joint proposal.

Central Purchasing an Aid to the Finance Department

The co-operation of the finance department has been most essential in making the work of the committee a success. The finance department at the comptroller's direction has given this co-operation freely and aided the committee in many ways.

Central purchasing has reduced materially the work on contract documents performed by the finance department for the several departments. Under the old plan of individual departmental contracts each bidder submitted a security deposit and afterwards, if successful, a security bond. Under the consolidated contract scheme one check has been submitted jointly for as many as fourteen departments at one time and one bond jointly for ten departments. According to the old plan bids were submitted on each separate departmental proposal. This year one joint bid has been submitted on proposals covering as many as ten, twelve, and fourteen departments at a time. In like manner joint security deposit transmission statements, and releases, rejection notices, waivers, advices of award, and finally joint contracts themselves have taken the place of the individual departmental document in each case. Consequently, all of these papers, which are handled and filed by the finance department, have been greatly reduced in number.

In addition to these advantages the number of bid openings to be attended by the finance department has been reduced, and the many questions which arise between the finance department and the various departments in the course of the award and execution of contracts can now be taken up in the majority of cases, as far as the mayor's departments are concerned, with a single department close at hand.

Material Reduction in Purchasing Work of Individual Departments

In addition to the many other ways cited in this report whereby individual departments are benefited by central purchasing, there has been a material reduction in the actual work of purchasing performed by these departments. While the departments still prepare contract estimates and assist in deciding the various important conditions entering into each new consolidated proposal, the greater part of the clerical work is now performed by the staff of the central purchasing committee. This work includes preparing the proposal, its printing and proof-reading, preparing the advertisement, issuing notifications to dealers, assembling and stamping proposals, the receipt and release of security deposits, the preparation of bid sheets and the tabulation of bids, the preparation of notices to dealers, advices of awards, notices of rejection, waivers, and finally the filling out of the contracts themselves, together with the transmission of all contract papers to and from the finance department. All of this work was formerly done by the individual departments. Now the departments only furnish the contract estimates and appropriation encumbrance figures, and give expert assistance in determining the contract conditions and in some cases in preparing the proposal. The central purchasing committee does the rest.

The number of departmental estimates furnished, and the accounting work of recording contracts, has been increased in the case of some departments, due to the fact that in previous years these particular departments have been accustomed to make annual contracts and combine many trade classes in a single proposal. On the other hand, many of the contracts issued by the committee have not exceeded a period of three months, and with one exception have covered only a single trade class. On account of the unsettled conditions of the market, however, short term contracts have been made necessary this year to secure the fullest amount of competition. A majority of the purchasing experts in the departments have felt that better competition could be further secured by advertising proposals for one trade class at a time.

Advantages to the Bureau of Standards

The bureau of standards, through its director, Mr. George L. Tirrell, a member of the mayor's committee, and Mr. R. Richmond Smith, chief of its supplies division, has co-operated with the committee in every way possible. On the other hand the work of the central committee has been of advantage to the bureau.

The bureau's work of securing the satisfactory use of its standard specifications has been simplified and aided through the joint proposals prepared by a single agency. It is obvious that a proposal containing seven or eight hundred separate items, most of which are covered by standard specifications, may easily fail to state for the information of dealers many of the details required by those specifications. The central purchasing committee found that a large part of its work in preparing the several contract proposals arose from the necessity of securing the requisite information from the departments to describe plainly the articles required and thereby meet the requirements of the standard specifications and of the trade as to completeness of detail.

Owing to the reduced number of proposals and contracts due to consolidation, the bureau of standards' work of examining and approving proposals and contracts as to their compliance with standard specifications has been greatly reduced. The committee's close contact with departments and dealers has enabled it to recommend beneficial changes in specifications which the bureau has always carefully considered and usually adopted.

The committee has afforded the bureau an opportunity to study at first hand the value of its specifications in actual operation, and to revise them promptly when found defective. Tentative specifications prepared by the bureau of standards have been given a trial in the committee's proposals, usually with results satisfactory to the departments requiring the articles covered thereby. Thus, in the proposal for pipe and pipe fittings, etc., about sixty-five tentative specifications were used covering pipe and pipe fittings, tools, hose, and several kinds of machinists' materials and supplies. In the proposal for household ware, tentative specifications were used covering decorated and undecorated china ware. In the proposal for clothing, drygoods and notions, tentative specifications were used covering oil clothing, oil squam hats and nurses' uniforms. In the proposal for photographic materials and supplies, a tentative specification covering X-ray plates was used for the requirements of the department of public charities, after consultation with the officials of that department.

A plan for closer co-operation has been arranged between the bureau and the committee whereby the former may more fully use the committee's contract proposals to work out and perfect standard specifications, and may come in direct contact through the committee with departments and dealers in the actual process of buying and selling under standards promulgated. The new plan will materially aid the committee in obtaining increased and a better class of competition, and in reducing the cost of supplies.

The joint proposals of the committee have reduced the bureau's work of issuing the many different kinds of specifications to the departments, and have decreased the number of printed specifications used. The committee has afforded the bureau a most convenient means of obtaining the consent of the mayor's departments to the elimination of samples and of standardizing the various items of supply not already standardized.

HISTORY OF CO-OPERATIVE CENTRALIZED PURCHASING FOR THE CITY OF NEW YORK

Initial Effort by New York Charter Commission

The first important effort to centralize the purchase of supplies for New York City was made in 1909 by the New York charter commission. In the Administrative Code prepared by that commission, but not passed by the legislature, there was proposed a bureau of supplies whose functions were to include not only the standardization of all supplies used by the city, but a comprehensive plan of central purchasing. Under this bureau of supplies there were to be established the following six divisions:

a Records of appropriations, to keep records of all appropriations for supplies and to supervise the preparation of contracts
b Estimates and requirements
c Proposals for bids
d Deliveries
e Classification and standards
f Inspection

Appointment of a Commission on the Standardization of Supplies

The utter lack of uniformity in making, recording and accounting for purchases of supplies by the city government, together with the wide variance in prices, led to the appointment in May, 1910, of a small commission on the standardization of supplies under the direction of the board of estimate and apportionment.

At the beginning of 1913 the commission on standardization was merged into the newly created bureau of standardization of supplies of the board of estimate and apportionment, which on April 4th, 1914, became the supplies division of the present bureau of standards. This bureau has performed a most valuable service to the city by carrying forward the standardization of supplies and the preparation of specifications for them, the use of which is now a mandatory condition attached to all appropriations for supplies, material and equipment. This work of standardization is only partially completed.

The Comptroller's Plan

In March, 1913, Comptroller William A. Prendergast submitted to the board of estimate a plan for a central purchasing department for supplies required by the city. He called attention to the fact that in the new Municipal Building there "will then be under one roof forty-eight purchasing officials, each engaged in buying practically the same kind of articles," and that "millions of dollars worth of supplies are purchased annually by the various departments at practically retail prices." He compared the methods then in use with those of a hundred small stores in no way connected with each other.

This plan provided for a board of purchase to be composed of the mayor, comptroller and president of the board of aldermen, and two executive officials, a "general purchasing agent" and a "general storekeeper." Each department was to be represented in the department of purchase by an assistant purchasing agent familiar with its needs. Departmental stores were to be maintained and were to be replenished from a general storehouse. All supplies required by city departments, except perishable supplies for daily delivery and coal, wood, and forage, were to be requisitioned by the general storekeeper and purchased for delivery once a month to the general city storehouse in the gross quantities required for the entire city.

Mayor Appoints Central Purchasing Committee

In November, 1914, Mayor Mitchel determined to attempt the actual work of central purchasing for the departments immediately under his direction without waiting further for legislation.

The central purchasing committee was thereupon appointed. With the exception of the executive secretary who was especially employed for this work, the staff utilized by the committee in its work was obtained, by arrangement, from the commissioners of accounts and from the purchasing divisions of the various departments.

The mayor decided that a successful beginning, at least, could be made preparatory to obtaining charter changes, and that the experimental organization could be developed into permanent form as soon as proper legislation was obtained.

PRESENT ORGANIZATION

The work of the central purchasing committee began in November, 1914, with one man and one room. Gradually a staff has been assembled adequate to care for a large part of the city's purchases.

At the outset it was determined to undertake the practical study of four problems:

1 Consolidation of all contract purchasing for the mayor's departments.

2 Consolidation of all open market order purchasing for the same departments.

3 Organization of a central clearing house to promote the transfer and disposal of dead and obsolete stock now lying dormant in the various departments.

4 Central control of the departmental sale of condemned articles.

While detailed plans have been drawn for the organization and promotion of the three latter lines of work and a beginning has been made on the consolidation of open market orders, the far greater part of the committee's efforts has been directed toward the consolidation of contract purchasing, this being considered the most difficult part of the plan to initiate.

This work is now organized in three divisions:

1 Executive
2 Administrative
3 Operative
    a Accounting and statistics
    b Contract preparation
    c Contract promotion
    d Contract award and execution

Each step in the procedure of purchasing under consolidated contracts is allotted to one of these divisions and to a definite man or group of men in a division as follows:

1 *EXECUTIVE*

5 men: Committee in general charge of entire work. (Part time).

2 *ADMINISTRATIVE*

1 man: In direct charge of all work and acting as secretary of the Committee.

3 *OPERATIVE*

a Accounting and Statistics

1 man: In charge of files, contract records, statistical records, etc.
2 men: Acting as messengers.

b Contract Preparation

1 man: In charge of all the work of this division and acting as assistant head of the department
2 men: Obtaining classified contract estimates from the various departments
Consolidating estimates preparatory to associate committee meetings
Holding committee conferences for the preparation of consolidated proposals
Preparing proposal copy for printer
19 men: Consolidating estimates, standardizing items (Part time) and preparing proposals

c Contract Promotion

1 man: In charge of all of the work of this division
Printing and mimeographing proposals
Care of samples and sample room.
1 man: Obtaining approval of bureau of standards and corporation counsel on proposals
In charge of mailing list
Advertising proposals
Notifying dealers of advertised proposals.
3 men: Reading proposal proof
Assembling and stamping proposals to be given out to dealers and finally as contracts

2 men: Blocking out tabulation sheets
Tabulating bids
Delivering certified tabulation sheets and copies of proposals to participating departments.

d Contract Award and Execution

1 man: In charge of all the work of this division, and the approval of all contract papers before transmission to the finance department.

1 man: Analyzing contract bids
Obtaining waivers from dealers on tie bids and preparing rejection notices for departments on rejected lines.

2 men: Obtaining incumbrance figures for advices of award
Preparing notices to contractors and advices of award
Obtaining signatures on awards and transmitting them to contractors and finance department.

4 men: Blockingout contracts and obtaining thereon signatures of contractors, bonding company and heads of interested departments
Transmission of contracts to finance department for certification
Transmission of executed contracts to dealers and departments.

Of this staff, 17 members were detailed from the office of the commissioners of accounts. The Bureau of Municipal Research assigned a member of its staff, and several men from the Training School for Public Service. The stenographic and mimeographing work of the committee is done in the offices of the commissioners of accounts. Nineteen of the best purchasing experts in the various departments have been made associate members of the central purchasing committee. The most experienced in each trade class of supplies and materials was appointed chairman of a sub-committee composed of three or four members most familiar with that particular class of supply. These committees prepare proposals, recommend awards and assist in every manner possible in the purchase of items within their class. The following chart shows the present organization of the work.

PRESENT PROCEDURE

Collection and Consolidation of Contract Estimates

Prior to the time for which contracts are asked, estimates are requested from the various departments for the class of supply, material or equipment which they desire to purchase. These estimates are submitted on uniform sheets prepared by the committee and are received and bound in the division of contract preparation. The items are listed on the estimates in accordance with a schedule

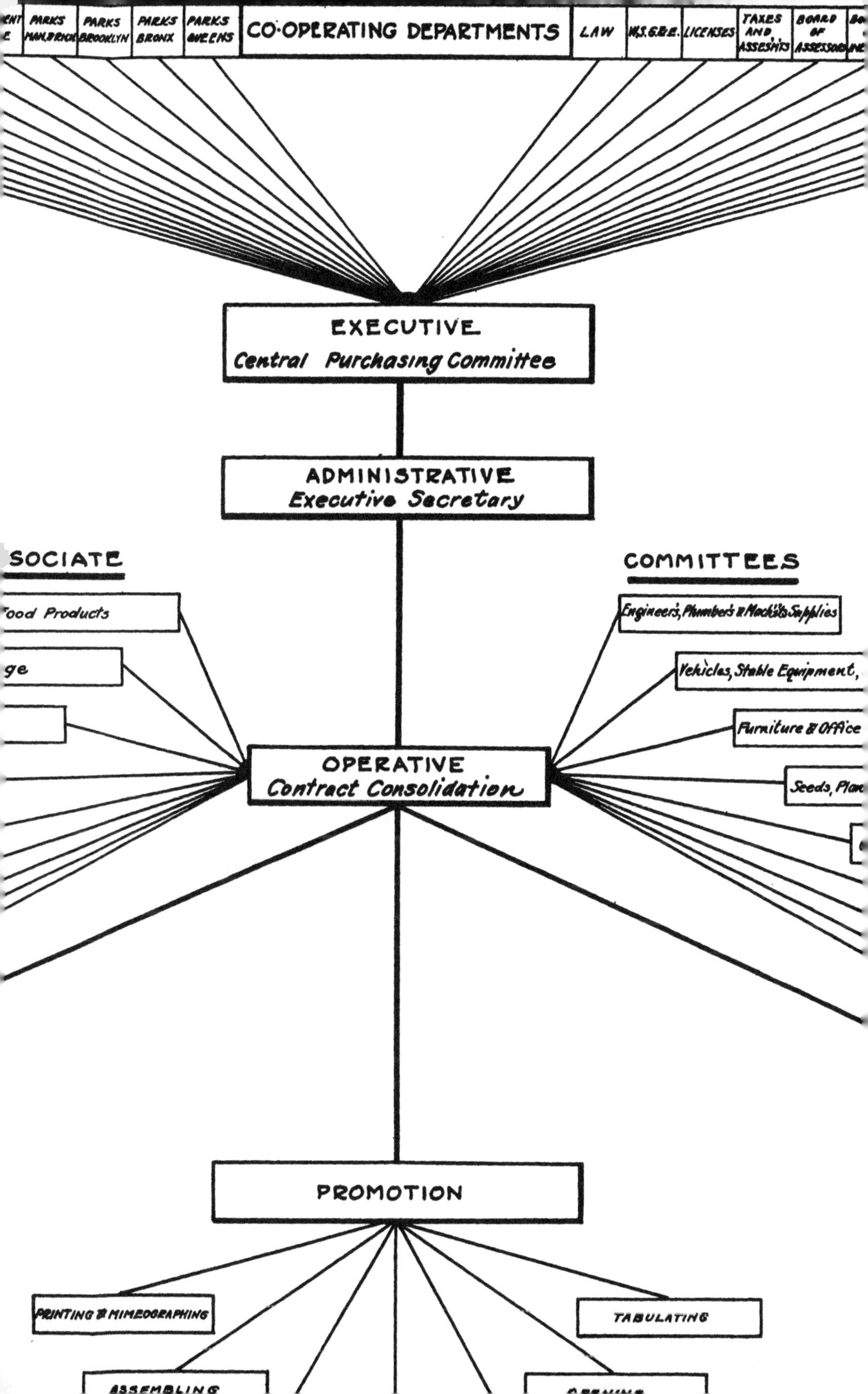

PARKS MAN. & RICH.
PARKS BROOKLYN
PARKS BRONX
PARKS QUEENS
CO-OPERATING DEPARTMENTS
LAW
W.S.G.& E.
LICENSES
TAXES AND ASSESM'TS
BOARD OF ASSESSORS
EXECUTIVE
Central Purchasing Committee
ADMINISTRATIVE
Executive Secretary
SOCIATE
COMMITTEES
Food Products
Engineers, Plumbers & Mach'sts Supplies
Vehicles, Stable Equipment,
Furniture & Office
Seeds, Plan
OPERATIVE
Contract Consolidation
PROMOTION
PRINTING & MIMEOGRAPHING
TABULATING

sent out by the committee, so that all items from each department will be listed in practically the same order. Various departmental estimates are then consolidated on one sheet and similar items for different departments are placed on the same line across the sheet.

Associate Committee Conferences

A meeting is held of the sub-committee on that class of supply, to which are invited, as a rule, dealers and a representative of the bureau of standards. Departments are induced to agree with each other on common items, containers and specifications, where no standards have previously been established. The term of the contract, the number of delivery points, the territory to be covered in each geographical district, special instructions to bidders, and all other items intended to make the proposal attractive to dealers and invite the lowest prices are worked out in these conferences.

Preparation of Contract Proposal

The results are then taken by the committee's staff and worded into a finished proposal ready for the printer. In preparing the proposal, and in committee conferences, all the weaknesses in proposals previously advertised for the same class and all the criticisms and suggestions previously received from dealers and departments, are taken into consideration, with the result that each succeeding proposal for the same class of supply is made stronger than those preceding it.

Advertisement of Proposal

The proposal is then turned over to the division of contract promotion, from which it is sent to the printer. After receiving the approval of the law department as to form, and of the bureau of standards as to specifications, it is advertised for a minimum period of ten days. During this time large numbers of dealers call for proposals at the offices of the committee, which affords splendid opportunity to obtain helpful criticisms and suggestions for the preparation of the next proposal. In addition to the published advertisement, written and telephonic notices of the proposal are sent out to a trade list of manufacturers, etc., composed of a consolidation of all departmental lists and of all other names that could be obtained from any other source.

Central Sample Room

The division of contract promotion is also charged with the care of samples. A central sample room for the city has been established in which many of the samples called for in the proposals are exhibited, thus enabling the prospective bidder to inspect samples in one central place.

Opening of Bids

Under the present law all departments interested in the proposal must be legally represented at the opening of bids. All openings are held at 12 o'clock noon and the bids are tabulated at once, so that at 3 P. M. of the same day, in practically every case, recommendations of award can be prepared by the purchasing agents of the various departments at a meeting held in the office of the committee.

Awards and Rejections

As soon as the bids have been tabulated and rechecked, certified copies of the tabulation sheets, with a copy of the proposal, are sent to each of the interested departments and to the division of contract award and execution. This division is charged with the responsibility of obtaining awards and rejections from the various departments on all the items of the proposal. It also secures waivers from dealers on tie items and on portions of items which departments have decided to reject.

Advices of Award

The bids are then analyzed according to dealers, and notices to contractors and advices of award prepared after the available appropriation balances have been obtained from each participating department. When these documents have been signed by the proper departmental officers they are sent to the contractor and finance department respectively, and the contractor is requested to submit his surety to the finance department for approval. At the time the advices are submitted to the various departments for signature, all of the necessary details are supplied to enable each department to make the proper book entries for its portion of the contract.

Preparation of Contract

While awaiting the return of the approval of surety from the finance department, the necessary copies of the contract are prepared in the office of the committee, so that as soon as the notice of approval is received, the contractor may be notified that his contract is ready for his signature and that of his bonding company. The supplies to be obtained from a single dealer by all of the departments participating in the joint proposal are consolidated in one contract.

Execution of Contract

After the signatures of the contractor and the bonding company have been obtained, in addition to those of the commissioner of each interested department, the contract is sent to the finance department for certification. Upon receipt of the notice of certification, a copy of the executed contract is sent to the contractor and to each of the participating departments.

Open Market Order Agreements

As a rule, whenever an award to a dealer is less than $1,000, an open market order agreement is entered into in place of a formal contract. No contract or advice of award is then prepared. A notice of award, however, signed by each department interested is sent to the successful bidder and a copy to each of the interested departments, stating that an agreement has been entered into on which open market orders may be drawn.

Security Deposits

Each time a bid is received, a certified check is submitted by the bidder as security for his bid. If the bidder is unsuccessful or receives an award of less than $1,000 this check is returned as soon as the advices of award are signed and sent to the finance department. If the bidder is successful, a release of his check is prepared by the committee as soon as his contract is signed by himself and his bonding company.

Time Record of Proposals and Contracts

Large record sheets are kept in the division of contract promotion and of contract award and execution, on which each new proposal and contract is respectively entered. There are 43 separate steps through which each proposal and contract must pass before final execution. Every step and signature in the proposal and contract procedure of each document is marked on the chart at the time it is made, so that at a glance the status of any proposal or contract may be easily ascertained.

Statistical Records

In addition to the above records, the following card records are maintained:

1 Card for each article purchased, giving all necessary data, including price, date, period, territory and departments covered.

2 Contract card, used as an index to the contract files and containing dates and data relating to the procedure of each contract to its execution.
3 Proposal card giving similar data relating to each proposal.
4 Contractor's card showing the volume of business transacted with each contractor.

General Contract Statistics

A large tally sheet is maintained on which general data relating to each proposal is entered for statistical purposes. This information includes the number, date and term of proposals issued, the number of bids received and contract and open market order agreements issued, the total value of the proposal and the values allotted to each interested department.

Contract Files

One copy of each executed contract is filed in the office of the committee. These contracts are numbered, indexed and filed in sets for each proposal. The first contract derived from a proposal is placed in a "king" file, and there is a serially numbered envelope for each of the other contracts connected with that proposal. All waivers, rejections, correspondence, advices, notices, etc., connected with any particular contract are filed in the envelope containing that contract, while all papers and correspondence connected with the proposal as a whole, including copies of advertisement, transmission and release of security deposits, etc., are filed in the "king" envelope. A separate file is maintained of copies of all contracts for supplies, etc., awarded by the mayor's departments individually during 1915. Files are maintained for departmental and outside correspondence, and for associate committee information. The latter is filed by trade classes, and contains current accumulating data and information to be used by the various sub-committees in the preparation of their next proposals.

DEFECTS IN THE PRESENT CITY PURCHASING SYSTEM

It has been apparent to everyone connected with the work of the mayor's committee that there are many defects in the present purchasing methods of the city which, if overcome, would greatly reduce the cost of supplies, materials and equipment, improve the service given by dealers and increase the quality of the articles delivered.

Summary of Defects

The following is a summary of some of the present handicaps to economical city purchasing:

1 Defects in the city charter in relation to purchasing.
2 Defects in the standard proposal and contract.
3 Lack of uniformity in the inspection of the same article by the various departments.
4 Failure to conform to the commercial practice of making prompt payment of claims.
5 Execution of contracts delayed by over-segregated appropriations.
6 Contracts delayed to obtain numerous signatures.
7 Waste in multiplicity of purchasing staffs.
8 Waste through inaccurate estimates and present form of contract defining the quantity to be delivered.
9 Compulsory awards to unreliable bidders.
10 Unnecessary multiplication of purchases due to failure to regulate requisitions.

Defects in Detail

A Defective City Charter

The city charter governing the methods of purchases gives the committee and the departments little latitude in the method to be used relative to each purchase to produce the most economical results. It provides minute details of contract procedure which are cumbersome and tend to red tape, delay and high prices.

Defects in Standard Proposal and Contract

The standard form of proposal and contract, in its present shape, tends to reduce competition and increase prices. For example, under the present standard proposal the only checks which are accepted by the finance department as legal security deposits with bids are those certified by a national, a state or a city bank of the City of New York. This restriction makes it very inconvenient for manufacturers in other cities to bid on city contracts, as cashiers' checks or checks certified by out-of-town banks submitted with the bid now make that bid informal. A number of low bids from reliable manufacturers have been lost during the year on this account. It is hoped that the law department, the bureau of standards and the committee will co-operate in revising these documents in 1916.

Lack of Uniformity in Departmental Inspection

The present system of individual departmental inspection is not uniform in its application by the various departments to similar deliveries from the same dealers, and therefore tends to confuse dealers and drive them away from bidding on city business. Different inspectors give the same specification different interpretations, so that while one department may accept a delivery of supplies, another may reject a delivery made from the same lot.

Failure in the Matter of Prompt Payment of Claims

There are exceptional delays on the part of several of the departments in passing bills for payment. They fail to conform to the commercial practice of making prompt payment of claims. Although the finance department has systematized its handling of claims so that they are now paid within an average of ten days after receipt from the original department, the city is rarely able to take advantage of cash discounts on account of the slow handling of claims by the average department receiving the supplies. Dealers in their attitude toward the city do not recognize individual departments, and defective inspection or abnormal delay in paying claims on the part of any single department tends to drive away some of the best sellers from the entire city business. Large manufacturers do not care to submit themselves to treatment of this character, and the best of the smaller dealers are often prevented from bidding because they have not sufficient capital to enable them to wait sixty days or more for payment. The centralization of departmental accounting processes in the department of finance will, it is expected, effectively remedy this condition.

Execution of Contracts Delayed by Over-Segregated Appropriations

Many departmental appropriations are so finely segregated on the basis of estimates prepared months in advance of the time of expenditure, that the consolidated contracts of the central purchasing committee are subjected continually to great delays in obtaining the departmental contract encumbrance figures needed in the preparation of contract papers. During the latter half of the year the committee's contracts have been further delayed by deficits in some of the appropriations against which the contracts had to be certified, when other appropriations in the same department for the same character of supply had large unencumbered balances. The fire and water departments, for example, each have over forty various appropriations for supplies, material and equipment divided not only by the character of the item but by its functional use. It has usually taken an average of three weeks officially to transfer funds from one appropriation to another. The centralizing of accounting will greatly facilitate the execution of joint contracts.

Contracts Delayed to Obtain Numerous Signatures

Owing to the present charter provisions requiring each department to do its own purchasing, the mayor's committee has been only an agency through which the departments could co-operate in obtaining prices on consolidated contract proposals. The committee has consequently been unable to relieve the commissioners and officials of the various departments of the details of attending bid openings, and of signing each and every one of the numerous documents connected with the execution of a contract. The necessity of obtaining these numerous signatures on all joint contract papers has still further delayed the central purchasing committee in the execution of its contracts. If these various delays can be overcome in 1916, the only present drawback to manufacturers, etc., in selling through the central committee as contrasted with the individual departments will be removed.

Waste in Multiplicity of Purchasing Staffs

The committee has until now confined its efforts almost entirely to contract purchasing. The mayor's departments are still buying individually on open market orders, necessitating the retention of the old purchasing staffs in each department. It has been estimated that there are at present approximately 120 purchasing agencies in the entire city government, and there are over 40 in the Municipal Building alone. At least 28 and probably all of these may be consolidated, if the work of the committee is continued.

Waste Through Inaccurate Estimates and Present Form of Contract Relating to Deliveries

Occasionally, departmental contract estimates are inaccurate owing to the absence of proper departmental consumption records, or to unexpected changes in institutional population, etc., after the estimates have been prepared. Under the present contract procedure the department purchasing supplies is compelled to certify in advance, against its appropriation, the exact contract value representing a specific quantity to be delivered. If the department has over-estimated it is only permitted to reduce the quantity called for by the contract by five per cent.; and if it has under-estimated, it may only increase the contract quantity five per cent.

Many purchasing departments both private and public outside of New York City state only approximate quantities in their contracts, and if the certification of the definite quantity against a fund is required that certification is made for a minimum amount, beyond which the department later may make such additional certifications as may be necessary. In New York City the departments are occasionally in the position of being compelled to take supplies that they do not need at a contract price in excess of the current market prices, or are compelled to buy supplies in the open market at higher prices when the quantity specified in a contract at a lower price has been completely delivered before the period of the contract has expired.

Compulsory Awards to Unreliable Bidders

At the present time departments are compelled to accept the lowest contract bidder on each item or class of supplies advertised unless that bidder happens to have defaulted on some previous contract.

The result is that often awards are made on bids which the other competing manufacturers believe are too low to permit deliveries in accordance with the contract specifications without a material loss of money. This happens in some items of supplies so systematically that it tends to cause legitimate dealers to withdraw from city competition. The natural results of bids of this character are that the departments have continual difficulty in obtaining deliveries from these habitual low bidders in accordance with the specifications and are greatly delayed in obtaining necessary supplies. Some provision should be made to permit the rejection of bids from dealers with whom departments have systematically had this experience.

Unnecessary Multiplication of Purchases Due to Failure to Regulate Requisitions

The large city departments issue many thousands of open market orders in a year. Very few departments have any plan in operation for reducing this large number of purchases. This means that there are no fixed periods intervening between the purchases of a specific class of supply. Requisitions for cleaning material, for example, would be accepted from the various bureaus, divisions or storehouses every day in the week and several times a day, if properly presented. There are no regularly recurring definite dates, which employees clearly understand are the only ones on which requests for the purchase of cleaning material will be accepted. This defective planning results in a large number of smaller purchases, fewer bids on account of the quantity being unattractive, higher prices, and a continuous waste of labor through the unnecessary multiplication of purchases.

Questionnaire Sent to Dealers

An endeavor is now being made, by means of a questionnaire to over 2,300 dealers with whom the committee has come in contact, to definitize the practical defects in the present purchasing system of the city. When the large number of replies already received have been tabulated under headings showing the various drawbacks to the widest competition, there should be enough convincing evidence to procure a marked improvement. These letters will be made the subject of a future report.

CONSTRUCTIVE OUTLINE OF AN EFFECTIVE PURCHASING SYSTEM FOR THE CITY OF NEW YORK

In the light of the experience derived from the past year's work the following constructive outline of an effective purchasing system is offered. In it an endeavor has been made to retain all of the advantages and to eliminate the defects in the present system of city purchasing. The plan is submitted with the hope that it may serve as a basis for conference and that it may aid the prompt establishment of central purchasing as a permanent agency in this city.

The support of the work by the staff of the commissioners of accounts is temporary and may be used only in the absence of any specific appropriation for central purchasing and while the work is in an experimental stage. Although this trained staff should be retained for some time, at least in part, specific appropriation should be made for the conduct of this work on an independent basis during the coming year. Under the plan submitted herewith, the new department should be installed and eventually operated without any additional cost to the city government.

In the consolidation at one time of all departmental purchases there is great danger of seriously interfering with the activities of the various departments. Consequently, the entire purchasing work of a few departments only should be taken over at the beginning, preferably those departments most familiar with the present work of consolidated purchasing. The following is a brief summary of the plan recommended, illustrated by the accompanying chart:

Supervising Board

1 A central purchasing department organized under a board similar to that of the city record. At a later period at least, if not at present, this board should assume the purchasing functions of the board of city record. The board

of city purchase should be composed of the following officials:

Mayor, chairman
Comptroller
Member of the board of estimate designated by that body
Two representatives at large appointed by the mayor

Director of Purchase

2 A director, or supervisor, appointed by the chairman of the board or by the board as a whole to be in direct charge of the department with full power to sign documents, execute contracts, open market orders, etc. An assistant director to be appointed by the director with the approval of the board, who should exercise all of the power of the director in the latter's absence.

Voluntary or Mandatory Participation

3 With the exception of the mayor's departments, participation in the scheme by other departments should be entirely voluntary or by order of the board of estimate and apportionment, after which time the purchases of those departments, should be as much under the direction of the head of the central purchasing department as those of any of the mayor's departments.

Purchasing Program for the First Year

4 As no central purchasing scheme is economical that provides for the retention of purchasing staffs in the individual departments as well as in the central department, and as it would be impracticable to undertake the purchase of all supplies, material, and equipment for a large number of departments at one time, all purchases of this character by Bellevue and allied hospitals and the departments of health, public charities and correction should be assumed by the central department on January 1, 1916, with the exception of a limited amount of emergency purchases which of necessity would have to be made by the individual departments but which should be confirmed immediately through the central department.

The clerical work of printing, advertising and executing contracts and open market orders for construction and repair work in these four departments should be assumed by the central department on the same date, but the proposal, specifications, drawings, etc., for contracts and open market orders of this character should continue to be prepared by the individual department.

In addition to assuming all of the contract and open market order buying of the above departments, the present program of consolidated contract purchases for all of the

BOARD OF CITY PURCHASE

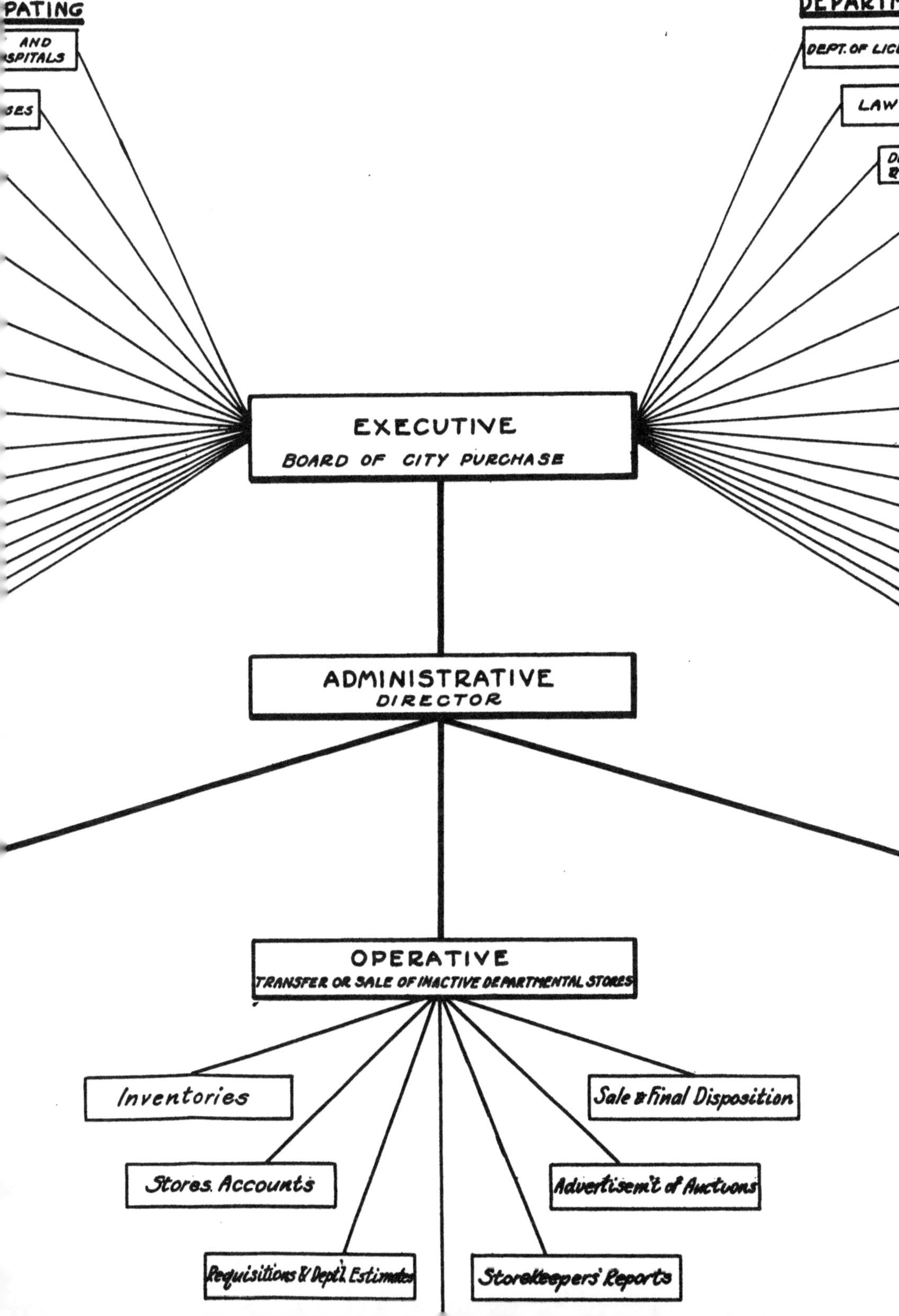

mayor's departments should be maintained and the entire purchasing work of these departments should be assumed by the central department, one or more departments at a time, as soon as the satisfactory operation of the original work undertaken would permit.

Composition of Central Purchasing Department Staff

5 Such part of the purchasing staffs of these four departments as may be required should be transferred to the payroll of the central department. As the work of many of these men at present includes duties other than those of purchasing, re-adjustments of duties in the individual departments in many cases would be necessary, but from each department the central department should obtain the services of at least four or five men. From unofficial estimates made in three of the departments affected, the number (including several stenographers) which could be transferred if this plan were adopted is approximately seven from each department. When all of the departments which would eventually participate in the plan had transferred their purchasing to the central department, the resultant central staff would be more than sufficient to maintain the work, and a material number of men would be released for other services in the various departments.

Until a sufficient part of the departmental purchasing staffs has been transfered to the central department to enable that department properly to conduct its work, the present staff of the commissioners of accounts now at work under the central committee should be retained, such detail being gradually reduced as men are transferred from other departments. By this method the establishment of a central department on a permanent basis would reduce the appropriation of the city for salaries for purchasing service before the end of the first year of operation.

Disposal of Staffs transferred from Departments

6 The men transferred from the participating departments would consist of three classes—purchasing agents, clerks, and stenographers. The two latter classes, as stated above, would gradually replace the staff now supplied by the commissioners of accounts. The former, while maintaining for a time the connection between the central department and their individual departments, to prevent the embarrassment of their respective departments in the retardation of purchasing service, would eventually become a staff of experts, each one on a particular class of supplies or materials, connected with the preparation of contract and open market order proposals. While at present these purchasing agents are engaged in purchasing all lines of supplies for their individual departments, by the method outlined above they would confine their ef-

forts to an intensive study of a single class, or of a few related classes. This plan would result in a material financial saving to the city.

Central Clearing House for Excessive and Obsolete Departmental Stock

7 It is not unusual for a department to purchase an article with which another department is overstocked. A central clearing house should be established as a part of the central department in which records should be maintained of departmental stores which any co-operating department finds difficult to use. Requests for supplies, etc. as received from the departments should be checked against these records and filled wherever possible from obsolete or excess stock of other departments, avoiding additional purchases. This plan would bring each department in current touch with available stores in all of the participating departments. When sufficient time had elapsed to demonstrate the uselessness of an article to all departments, the central department should see to its sale to the advantage of the city.

Centralized Inspection in the Finance Department

8 One of the defects and drawbacks in the present plan of purchasing is lack of uniformity and justice in the present system of departmental inspection. The city is also now maintaining two complete staffs of inspectors, one in the departments, and one in the finance department, both doing practically the same work. We believe the present situation would be bettered, if inspection by the departments were abolished, and the entire responsibility for inspection of deliveries centered in the finance department. We believe that there is no necessity for the present double check on deliveries, for if the inspection of the finance department prove ineffective in any respect, complaints would soon be heard from those actually using the supplies, etc., in the departments.

Close Relation of Standardization of Supplies to Purchasing

9 Standard specifications for supplies and materials cannot be established satisfactorily by a department not in close touch with the actual purchase of these articles. A sufficient number of experts should be detailed to the central department from the bureau of standards, supply division, on January 1, 1916, to put together the specifications for all contracts and open market orders, and to meet the hundreds of dealers and departmental officials and employees with whom the central department comes in daily contact. This would serve to determine the relative effectiveness and value of existing specifications with a view to their beneficial revision.

Appropriation for a Central Purchasing Department

10 A sufficient appropriation for the current expense of the central department should be provided by the city for the year 1916. During the year, as other departments participated fully in the scheme and their purchasing staffs were transferred to the central department, the corresponding sum in the appropriations of the individual department should also be transferred. Under this plan the only original appropriation for salaries and wages that would have to be made for the central department on January 1, 1916, would be for a director, an assistant director, chief purchasing clerk, and messengers. The following is a suggested original appropriation based on the above plan, including tentative salary schedules:

Personal Service—			
Salaries, Regular Employees—			
Director		$5,000.00	
Assistant Director		3,000.00	
Clerk (Purchasing Agent)		2,500.00	
Clerks, 4 at $300		1,200.00	
Total Personal Service			$11,700.00
Supplies—			
Office Supplies		$700.00	
Postage		600.00	
Trade papers and books		100.00	
Total Supplies			1,400.00
Purchase of Equipment—			
Furniture		$520.00	
Typewriters		400.00	
Calculating machines		780.00	
Total Purchase of Equipment			1,700.00
Contract or Open Order Service—			
General Repairs—			
Repairs to furniture and equipment		$100.00	
Transportation—			
Carfare	$300.00		
Express, freight, etc.	50.00		
		350.00	
Communication—			
Telephone and Telegraph		1,000.00	
Total Contract or Open Order Service			1,450.00
Contingencies			250.00
Departmental Total			$16,500.00

A Central Supply Fund

11 Probably the greatest hindrance to the present experiment of consolidated contracting is the number of signatures which have to be obtained from various departments on each document. This is not only annoying to the heads of the various departments but is a great cause of delay to the central department in executing contracts. To obviate this defect, as soon as necessary charter changes are obtained, a central supply fund should be established under the central department with specific amounts allotted therein for supplies, materials, and equipment.

In the case of departments not fully participating in the plan, the original appropriations for supplies, etc., should be made to the individual departments, but when legal authority is obtained advances should be made by transfer through the board of estimate and apportionment to the central supply fund sufficient to cover any consolidated contracts under preparation for those departments. These transfers of advances would be repeated at various times throughout the year until the central department took over all of the purchasing of any individual department, when the entire balance of that department's appropriation for supplies, etc., should be transferred to the central fund.

Under this plan contract and open market order documents could be certified against the various allotments of the central fund and signed by the director or supervisor of the central department.

Suggested Organization and Duties

12 The new department should be organized for the present in three divisions as follows:

- A Executive
- B Administrative
- C Operative
  - 1 Preparation, promotion and execution of contracts and open market orders.
  - 2 Transfer or sale of inactive departmental stores.
  - 3 Accounting.

A EXECUTIVE

The executive division should consist of the board of purchase which should have general supervision over the entire work, and appoint the director.

B ADMINISTRATIVE

The administrative division should consist of the director and his assistants. They should have charge of the active direction of the work and have the power to open bids, make awards and sign contract and open market order papers. The assistants and all other employees should be appointed by the director with the approval of the board.

C OPERATIVE

1 *Preparation, Promotion and Execution of Contracts and Open Market Orders*

The contract and open market order division should be under the direct charge of the head of the division, subject to the general supervision of the director. The purchasing agents transferred from the various individual departments would be attached to this division as purchasing agents and specialists in specific classes of supplies. The division should be divided into three sections, as follows, each one in charge of an employee under the direction of the head of the division.

a The Preparation of Contracts and Open Market Order Proposals

This section should be charged with the duty of collecting periodically contract and open market order estimates and requisitions from the various participating departments, and with the scientific consolidation of these estimates and requisitions in the form of contract and open market order proposals. In case greater latitude is ever given to the city in the method of buying, this section should also undertake the promulgation of continuing price agreements. To obtain the best results for the city the central department should be left free to choose in the case of each purchase the method of buying which would produce the greatest economy. The various purchasing experts transferred from the individual departments would be attached to this section as purchasing agents of special classes of supplies, in accordance with the plan outlined above.

b Promotion of Contract and Open Market Order Proposals

This section should be charged with the duty of printing, assembling and advertising contract proposals, notifying manufacturers, etc., of bid openings, opening and tabulating bids and maintaining and exhibiting samples.

c Award and Execution of Contracts and Open Market Orders

This section should be charged with the duty of recommending awards on contracts and open market order bids, analysing contract bids, and preparing and obtaining the execution of all contract and open market order papers.

2 *Transfer or sale of Inactive Departmental Stores*

The head of this division under the supervision of the director should be charged with the duty of maintaining current records of all inactive supplies, materials, and equipment located in the various co-operating departments; checking contract estimates and open market order requisitions against these records before additional purchases are made; arranging for the transfer of articles from a department not needing them to the requisitioning department; and conducting the sale of inactive supplies, etc., which could not be used by any department.

3 *Accounting*

The head of the accounting division should be under the supervision of the director, and should be charged with the maintenance of the local accounting records of the central purchasing department, all records of contracts and open market orders and the necessary statistical records in relation to prices obtained, volume and classification of business, etc. The central department should depend upon the finance department for current statements of the unencumbered balances in the various departmental allotments from the general supply fund.

Contract Estimates and Open Market Requisitions

13 All estimates for contracts and requisitions for open market orders should continue to be prepared in the individual departments. While supporting data relating to stock on hand, average consumption, etc., should be required to be submitted with these estimates and requisitions, no attempt should be made by the central department, during its first year of operation at least, to control or check the accuracy of these estimates, if they are in accord with supporting data submitted, and if the attached certificates as to accuracy and necessity are properly signed. While the importance of this verification is recognized and appreciated, we believe that its establishment should be left to a later period in the development of the central department.

Contracts and Open Market Orders

14 All contracts and open market orders should be prepared and signed in the central department. The latter should be issued to the vendor through the finance department, in accordance with the new procedure proposed to be installed by that department on January 1, 1916. All contracts executed would be of the consolidated type, but all open market orders and claim vouchers would be prepared separately for each department and appropriation in accordance with the proposed new procedure laid down by the finance department.

Final Procedure

Although fully recognizing the direct bearing of central control over the storage and distribution of departmental stores on the success of a central purchasing system, we believe that enough work has been outlined in the above plan to engage the full time of the central department for at least a year, if the plan submitted is to be successfully installed, and that no additional work may be immediately undertaken without jeopardizing the success of the main plan.

If the suggestions submitted meet with approval, we recommend that they be at once submitted to the law department for advice as to what, if any, charter or ordinance changes should be made. If the plan in any respect conflicts with existing laws and ordinances, and if such conflict cannot be removed by feasible changes in the plan proposed, we would request that the law department proceed at once to draft the necessary legislation. Pending legislation, we believe that with the aid of the revised accounting procedure under way by the finance department and the experience gained from the past work of the mayor's committee, the present co-operative plan, modified as herein suggested, should be continued in effect. In this way efficient and practical central purchasing will be progressively achieved.

Respectfully Submitted,

HENRY BRUÈRE, Chairman,
GEORGE L. TIRRELL,
DAVID FERGUSON,
JAMES McGINLEY,
FREDERIC R. LEACH, Secretary,

Mayor's Central Purchasing Committee.

www.ingramcontent.com/pod-product-compliance
Lightning Source LLC
LaVergne TN
LVHW010623110826
845149LV00003B/1032

* 9 7 8 1 4 1 8 1 8 6 8 2 1 *